WONDROUS FOLK
COLORING BOOK

Christine Karron

WONDROUS FOLK
COLORING BOOK

This printing 2026
Copyright © 2025 Christine Karron

All rights reserved. Other than for personal use, no part of this book may be reproduced in any way, in whole or part, without the written consent of the copyright holder or publisher. We respectfully request that this content not be used to train AI-generative models or machine learning systems without the publisher's written consent.

Published by Blue Angel Publishing®
10 Trafford Court, Wheelers Hill
Victoria, Australia 3150

info@blueangelonline.com
blueangelonline.com

By Christine Karron

Edited by Cherise Asmah

Designed by Gemma Christensen

Blue Angel Publishing is a registered trademark of Blue Angel Gallery Pty. Ltd.

ISBN: 978-1-922574-38-1

Printed on sustainably sourced paper, with soy-based inks.

WONDROUS WELCOME

Given the success of my previously published coloring book, for which I received tons of positive feedback and requests for more books like *Wildflower Folk*, the decision to put together another coloring book was not a hard one.

Let me present to you this magical *Wondrous Folk* coloring book, featuring 50 of my most popular and beloved illustrations, plus four new exclusive illustrations: *Christmas Joy, Marigold, Wind of Change* and *Witches' Magic*, which I drew specifically for this book.

In this book, you will find many different Fae and fantasy-realm-inspired, close-up portrait illustrations of marvellous female (and a few male) characters.

I have always been fascinated with drawing faces. In fact, I started doing portrait commissions when I was a teenager. Over the decades, I have found fulfillment in creatively drawing characters from my imagination with my own little twist.

May all the unique personalities and different faces in this book bring you many hours of peaceful coloring joy.

Christine Karron

AMONG DRAGONS

ANGEL

AQUA

ASTRAL FAE

BELLZ

BELOVED

CHRISTMAS JOY

CLEO

DAHLIA

DREAM WEAVER

ESMERALDA

FAE MESSENGERS

FAIRY BRIDE

FAIRY MAGIC

FAIRY PORTAL

FLOURISH FAE

FLOWER EARRING

FREE FALLING

FROST

GENIE

GRACE FAIRY

HYDRANGEA

JEWEL THIEF

JOYS OF SUMMER

MAE

MARIGOLD

MERMAID'S HEART

MESSAGE IN THE BOTTLE

MIDNIGHT ENCHANTRESS

MONA

NALA

NIXIE

NOVA

ODETTE

ONYX

ORCHID DREAM

OVER THE ROOFTOPS

OWL SHIFTER

QUEEN'S CHALICE

RAVEN GUIDE

SAMBA DANCER

SEA PEARLS

SNOWY TRAIL

STEAMPUNK HUNTRESS

STELLA

STRAWBERRY DREAM

SUGAR SKULL

SWEET TEMPTATION

TAROT READER

TRANQUIL GRACE

TRANSIENCE

VIOLA

WIND OF CHANGE

WITCHES' MAGIC

For more information on this or
any Blue Angel Publishing® release,
please visit our website at:

www.blueangelonline.com